CHRISTMAS AT HOME
WITH
Mary&Martha

Bakin' Up Cookies
& Love

BARBOUR
PUBLISHING

© 2006 by Barbour Publishing, Inc.

ISBN 1-59789-430-3

Recipes were compiled from the following titles, all published by Barbour Publishing, Inc.: *Heart's Delight*, *Homemade Christmas Cookies*, *Holiday Desserts*, *Holiday Jar Mixes*, *No-Bake Holiday Recipes*, *Traditional Christmas Favorites*, *101 Christmas Recipe Ideas*, *Holiday Snacks and Appetizers*, and *Homemade Christmas Sweets*.

Cover Design by Greg Jackson, Thinkpen Design, LLC.
Cover and Interior artwork by Karen M. Reilly

Published by Barbour Publishing, Inc., P.O. Box 719, Uhrichsville, Ohio 44683, www.barbourbooks.com

Our mission is to publish and distribute inspirational products offering exceptional value and biblical encouragement to the masses.

Member of the
Evangelical Christian
Publishers Association

Printed in Canada.
5 4 3 2 1

CONTENTS

*Love is patient, love is kind. It does not envy, it does not boast, it is not proud. It is not rude,
it is not self-seeking, it is not easily angered, it keeps no record of wrongs.
Love does not delight in evil but rejoices with the truth.
It always protects, always trusts, always hopes, always perseveres.*

1 CORINTHIANS 13:4–7

Meet Mary & Martha. . .

If you enjoy the delicious aroma of fresh-baked Christmas cookies coming from your kitchen, then this holiday cookbook is just for you. Featuring everything from traditional cutouts to easy no-bakes and jar mixes, and everything in between—if it'll make your holiday celebrations a little sweeter, it's in here!

We'll be appearing throughout the book, offering you tips and inspiration to make your Christmas just a bit merrier—and more meaningful.

Ready to bake up some cookies and love this season? Roll up your sleeves, put on that apron, and. . .
Happy cooking!

With love (from our kitchen to yours),
Mary & Martha

Fun to Cut
&
Decorate Cookies

*Blessed is the season which engages
the whole world in a conspiracy of love.*
HAMILTON WRIGHT MABI

Brown Sugar Cookies

2 cups light brown sugar
1 cup butter, melted
3 eggs
¼ cup milk
1 tablespoon vanilla
1 teaspoon baking soda
5 to 5½ cups flour

Mix ingredients in order given. Add just enough flour to make dough firm enough to roll.
Cut into shapes as desired. Decorate with colored sugars or sprinkle lightly with brown
sugar. Bake at 350° for 8 to 10 minutes or until edges are lightly browned.

Thank You, Lord, for the gift of Your love. May I be a shining example of that love to others this holiday season.

Butterscotch Gingerbread Men

½ cup butter, softened
½ cup brown sugar, packed
1 (3.4 ounce) package
   butterscotch instant pudding
1 egg

1½ cups flour
1½ teaspoons ginger
½ teaspoon baking soda
½ teaspoon ground cinnamon

Cream butter, brown sugar, and pudding mix. Add egg. Combine flour, ginger, baking soda, and cinnamon; gradually add to creamed mixture. Cover and refrigerate overnight. On a lightly floured surface, roll out dough to ⅛-inch thickness. Cut with 5-inch gingerbread man cutter. Place 1 inch apart on ungreased baking sheets. Bake at 350° for 8 to 10 minutes or until edges are golden. Remove to wire racks to cool, then decorate.

ICING:

2 cups powdered sugar
3 tablespoons milk

Assorted decorator candies
Raisins

Combine powdered sugar and milk until smooth.
Frost and decorate cookies with candies and raisins.

For lots of fun and great results, let your kids "paint" their own cookies. Make paint by mixing food coloring with egg yolks. Use brand-new paintbrushes and let the kids paint pictures on the cookies before baking. After baking, the colors will come out bright and glossy.

Christmas Stars

¾ cup butter, softened
1 cup sugar
2 eggs
1 teaspoon vanilla
2½ cups flour

1 teaspoon baking powder
¼ teaspoon salt
¼ cup green decorator sugar
  (optional)
6 tablespoons strawberry jam

In large bowl, cream butter and sugar until light and fluffy. Gradually add eggs and vanilla. Mix well. Sift together flour, baking powder, and salt. Stir flour mixture into butter mixture until well blended. Refrigerate dough for 3 hours. Preheat oven to 350°. Grease several cookie sheets. On floured surface, roll out half of dough at a time to ⅛-inch thickness. Cut dough into star shapes using 3- to 4-inch star cookie cutter. Using 1- to 2-inch star cookie cutter, cut stars into centers of half of the big stars. If desired, sprinkle colored sugar on cookies with center cut out. Place 1 inch apart on prepared cookie sheets and bake for 6 to 8 minutes. After cookies cool completely, spread 1 teaspoon jam in center of each cookie without center cut out. Place cookie with cutout on top of jam layer.
Pack cookies in covered tin to preserve freshness.

Chocolate Holiday Cookies

⅔ cup powdered sugar
½ cup butter or margarine, softened
½ teaspoon vanilla

1 cup flour
2 tablespoons cocoa
⅛ teaspoon salt

Beat together powdered sugar, butter, and vanilla at medium speed. Reduce speed and add flour, cocoa, and salt. Divide dough in half, refrigerating second half until ready to use. One half at a time, place dough between sheets of lightly floured waxed paper and roll out to ⅛-inch thickness. Remove paper and cut with 2- to 2½-inch cookie cutters. Place on ungreased cookie sheets. Bake at 325° for 14 to 18 minutes. Repeat process with second half of dough. Cool cookies completely before decorating with icing as desired.
Makes about 2 dozen cookies.

Icing:

1¼ cups powdered sugar
1 tablespoon meringue powder

2 tablespoons warm water
¼ teaspoon cream of tartar

Combine icing ingredients and beat at low speed until moistened. Increase speed and beat until stiff and glossy. Add more warm water if icing becomes too stiff.
Cover with damp paper towel until ready to use.

Christmas Tree Spice Cookies

1 cup butter
1 cup sugar
1 large egg
½ cup honey
¾ teaspoon baking powder

2 teaspoons ginger
4½ cups flour
½ teaspoon salt
1 teaspoon cinnamon
Colored sugar (optional)

Cream butter and sugar. Add egg and honey; continue beating until light and fluffy.
Mix in dry ingredients (except colored sugar). Cover and chill dough for 1 hour.
Roll out dough to ¼-inch thickness. Cut with 3- to 3½-inch tree-shaped cookie cutter.
Place on lightly greased cookie sheets. Sprinkle with colored sugar.
Bake at 375° for 10 to 12 minutes or until cookies are golden.

Eggnog Cookies

1 cup butter or margarine,
softened
2 cups sugar
1 cup eggnog

1 teaspoon baking soda
½ teaspoon nutmeg
5½ cups flour

Beat butter and sugar until fluffy. Add eggnog, baking soda, and nutmeg; mix well.
Gradually add flour, mixing well. Divide dough in half; wrap in plastic. Chill overnight
in refrigerator or 2 hours in freezer. On floured surface, roll out half of dough to ⅛-inch
thickness. Cut out with flour-dipped cookie cutters. Place 1 inch apart on ungreased
baking sheets. Bake at 375° for 8 to 10 minutes or until lightly browned.
Cool completely, then ice and decorate.

ICING:

3 cups powdered sugar
¼ cup butter or margarine, softened

⅓ cup eggnog

Beat powdered sugar and butter until well blended.
Gradually beat in eggnog until icing is smooth.

French Christmas Cookies

½ cup butter or other shortening, softened
¾ cup sugar
½ cup honey
2 egg yolks
¼ cup milk
1 teaspoon vanilla
3 cups flour, sifted

Cream butter and sugar together until light. Add honey and egg yolks, beating well after each addition. Add milk and vanilla. Add flour in small amounts until well blended. Chill dough for 2 hours. Roll out to ⅛- inch thickness on lightly floured board. Cut into desired shapes and bake on ungreased cookie sheets at 375° for 10 minutes. Cool and frost if desired. Makes 3 dozen.

Baking a variety of cookies? Be sure to store each properly. Don't store your moist bars with your crisp cookies. Soft cookies should be stored in an airtight container. Crisp cookies do well under a loose-fitting cover that allows moisture to escape. Bar cookies can be cut when cooled and kept in their baking pan under a foil cover until you are ready to serve them.

Gingerbread People

4 cups flour
1 tablespoon cinnamon
2 teaspoons baking powder
1½ teaspoons ginger
1½ teaspoons ground cloves
1 teaspoon baking soda
1 teaspoon nutmeg

1 teaspoon salt
1 cup unsalted butter
 (not margarine), softened
1 cup sugar
2 large eggs, separated
1 cup molasses
1 tablespoon cold water

OPTIONAL DECORATIONS:
Currants for eyes
Strips of candied cherries for smiles
Red hot cinnamon candies for buttons

Onto piece of waxed paper, sift 3¾ cups flour, cinnamon, baking powder, ginger, cloves, baking soda, nutmeg, and salt. In large bowl with electric mixer on high, cream butter and sugar until light yellow and fluffy. Beat in egg yolks one at a time, then molasses. Using wooden spoon, stir in flour mixture.
Cover and refrigerate dough for at least 1 hour or overnight.

(cont.)

18

Preheat oven to 350°. Butter three cookie sheets. On pastry cloth or board, sprinkle remaining ¼ cup flour and roll out half of dough to ¼-inch thickness. With cookie cutters, cut out gingerbread people. With spatula, transfer cookies to baking sheets. Decorate with currants, cherries, and cinnamon candies if desired. Whisk egg whites with water. Bake cookies for 5 minutes, then brush lightly with egg white mixture. Bake 2 to 3 minutes longer. Let cool on cookie sheets for 2 minutes. (To make holes for hanging, pierce top of each cookie with a skewer as soon as it comes out of the oven.) Transfer to racks to cool. Repeat with remaining dough and flour. Cool and decorate as desired.

ICING:

2½ cups powdered sugar, sifted
½ teaspoon vanilla
3 to 4 tablespoons cold water
Assorted food coloring

In small bowl, stir sugar with vanilla, then add enough water to make stiff icing. Divide into small cups and color as you wish. When cookies are cold, pipe out designs, such as smiling faces, zigzags, bow ties, and aprons. If using different colors of icing, let one color dry before piping next. Store cookies in airtight container for up to 2 weeks. Do not freeze, as icing could crack.

Holly Berry Cookies

2 cups flour
1 cup sugar
1 teaspoon cinnamon
¾ teaspoon baking powder
¼ teaspoon salt
½ cup butter, chilled
1 egg
¼ cup milk
⅔ cup seedless raspberry jam

In large bowl, combine flour, sugar, cinnamon, baking powder, and salt. Cut in butter until mixture resembles coarse crumbs. In small bowl, beat egg and milk. Add to crumb mixture until dough is moistened. Cover and refrigerate for at least 1 hour. Preheat oven to 375°. On lightly floured surface, roll out dough to ⅛-inch thickness. Cut with 2-inch round cookie cutter. Place on ungreased baking sheets. Bake for 8 to 10 minutes or until edges are lightly browned. Cool on wire racks. Once cool, spread jam on half of cookies, then top each with another cookie.

(cont.)

GLAZE:
2 cups powdered sugar
2 tablespoons milk
½ teaspoon vanilla
¼ cup red hot cinnamon candies
4 drops green food coloring

Combine powdered sugar, milk, and vanilla until smooth. Spread glaze over cookies and decorate with cinnamon candies before glaze is set. Let dry. Using small, new paintbrush and green food coloring, paint holly leaves on cookies.

Lemon Cinnamon Cookies

4 cups flour
2 cups sugar
1 tablespoon cinnamon
1 teaspoon cream of tartar
1 teaspoon baking soda
½ teaspoon salt
1 cup unsalted butter
3 eggs, beaten

2 teaspoons lemon zest
1 egg white
1 tablespoon water
Sugar
⅔ cup (4 ounces) semisweet
   chocolate chips, melted

In very large mixing bowl, stir together flour, sugar, cinnamon, cream of tartar, baking soda, and salt. Cut in butter until mixture looks like cornmeal. Add eggs and lemon zest; mix well to form dough. On floured surface, roll out dough to ⅛-inch thickness. Cut into shapes with cookie cutters. Place on ungreased cookie sheets. Combine egg white and water; brush over tops of cookies. Sprinkle cookies with sugar. Bake at 375° for 8 to 10 minutes or until golden. Remove to wire racks to cool. Drizzle melted chocolate over top. Cool before storing.

Lightly coat cookie cutters—especially plastic ones—with oil spray to keep them from sticking to the cookie dough.

Raisin-Filled Sugar Cookies

2 cups margarine
4 cups sugar
2 shakes nutmeg
2 teaspoons vanilla
6 eggs
½ teaspoon salt

4 teaspoons baking powder
12 cups flour
2 cups buttermilk
2 teaspoons baking soda
2 teaspoons lemon juice

Cream together margarine, sugar, nutmeg, vanilla, and eggs until blended. Combine salt, baking powder, and flour; set aside. Pour buttermilk in separate container; add baking soda and stir, then add lemon juice. Alternately add buttermilk mixture and flour mixture to butter mixture until thoroughly mixed. Roll out and cut with large cookie cutter. Put 1 tablespoon filling on each cookie and cover with another cookie. Bake at 400° for 15 to 20 minutes.

FILLING:

2 large boxes raisins
4 cups water

1 cup sugar
¼ cup flour

In blender, chop raisins in water, then cook with sugar and flour to thicken. Cool.

Shortbread Cutouts

1 cup butter, softened
½ cup sugar
2 cups flour, sifted

Cream butter and sugar until fluffy. Add flour and knead until dough breaks smoothly.
If extra flour is needed, add in small amounts. Roll out to ¼-inch thickness and cut into
shapes with cookie cutters. Bake at 350°for 12 to 15 minutes or until
slightly golden brown on top.

*Hold God's love in your heart—
and spread His love to others
this holiday season.*

❖ *Deliver a plate of your delicious
cutouts to a lonely neighbor.*

❖ *Invite an acquaintance to your
Christmas Eve church service.*

❖ *Donate Christmas gifts and food to
a needy family.*

❖ *Offer your babysitting services to
parents in need of a night out.*

❖ *Shovel snow for an elderly couple.*

❖ *Volunteer your free time in a soup
kitchen or for another worthy
cause.*

Sour Cream Christmas Cookies

1 cup shortening
1 cup margarine
2 cups sugar
2 eggs
2 teaspoons baking soda
¾ teaspoon salt
1 teaspoon baking powder

2 teaspoons vanilla
1 teaspoon lemon juice
1 teaspoon nutmeg
6 cups flour
1 cup sour cream
1 cup buttermilk

Melt shortening and margarine together; cream with sugar, eggs, baking soda, salt, and baking powder. Add vanilla, lemon juice, and nutmeg. Alternately add flour, sour cream, and buttermilk. Chill overnight, uncovered. Roll and cut on floured surface. Bake at 375° for 5 to 8 minutes or until soft in middle.

Sugar Cookies

⅔ cup butter
¾ cup sugar
1 egg
1 teaspoon vanilla
4 teaspoons milk
¼ teaspoon salt
1½ teaspoons baking powder
2 cups flour

Cream butter and sugar until fluffy. Blend in egg, vanilla, and milk. Add dry ingredients and mix well. Divide dough in half and chill for 1 hour. Roll out dough to ⅛-inch thickness on lightly floured surface and cut with cookie cutters, or roll into tube and slice. Bake at 375° for 6 to 8 minutes or until edges begin to brown.

Velvet Cutout Cookies

2 cups butter, softened
1 (8 ounce) package cream
  cheese, softened
2 cups sugar

2 egg yolks
2 teaspoons vanilla
4½ cups flour
¼ teaspoon salt

In large mixing bowl, cream together butter, cream cheese, and sugar until light and fluffy. Add egg yolks and vanilla; mix well. Gradually stir in flour and salt. Chill for 2 hours. Roll out dough on floured surface and cut into desired shapes. Place on greased baking sheets and bake at 350° for 9 to 12 minutes. Cool on cookie sheets before removing to wire racks. Frost if desired.

FROSTING:

4 tablespoons butter, softened
1 (3 ounce) package cream cheese,
  softened
3 cups powdered sugar, divided

3 tablespoons milk
½ teaspoon vanilla
Food coloring (optional)

In mixing bowl, beat together butter, cream cheese, and 1 cup powdered sugar until smooth. Add in milk and vanilla. Gradually mix in remaining powdered sugar and beat until smooth and spreadable. Divide frosting and tint with food coloring if desired.

Delightful Drop Cookies

Let us remember that the Christmas heart is a giving heart,
a wide open heart that thinks of others first.
GEORGE MATTHEW ADAMS

Angel Cookies

1 angel food cake mix
½ cup water
1 (8 to 12 ounce) bag dried mixed fruit, finely chopped

Combine cake mix and water. Stir in fruit. Line cookie sheet with foil. Drop dough by teaspoonfuls on foil. Bake at 400° for 8 to 10 minutes until puffy and golden in color. Cool well before trying to remove from foil.

HINT FOR SHIPPING CHRISTMAS COOKIES:

Bar cookies and drop cookies—such as plain chocolate chip and peanut butter—travel best. Frosted and filled cookies may soften and stick together. Cool cookies completely before packing. Carefully pack the cookies between layers of waxed paper in a tin, empty coffee can, or rigid box. Pack a piece of apple or slice of bread with soft cookies to keep them fresh. Use crumpled waxed paper or plain popcorn to fill in any open space. There should be no room for the cookies to shift. Pack this tin or box in a larger, sturdy shipping box. Pad the area around the tin or box with crumpled paper or other packing material, then seal and address. Be sure to write "Perishable" on the box.

Best Date Cookies

1 cup brown sugar
⅔ cup butter or ⅓ cup butter and ⅓ cup shortening
1 egg
1 teaspoon salt
1 teaspoon baking soda
¼ cup milk
2 cups flour
1 cup dates, chopped
½ cup nuts, chopped

Mix together all ingredients and drop onto ungreased cookie sheets.
Bake at 375° for 15 minutes.

Butterfinger Cookies

¾ cup sugar
½ cup butter, softened
1 large egg
1¾ cups flour
¾ teaspoon baking soda
¼ teaspoon salt
1 cup (about three 2.1-ounce bars) Butterfinger candy bars, coarsely chopped

Beat sugar and butter in large mixing bowl until creamy. Beat in egg. Combine flour, baking soda, and salt; gradually beat into egg mixture. Stir in Butterfinger pieces. Drop by slightly rounded tablespoons onto ungreased baking sheets. Bake at 375° for 10 to 12 minutes or until lightly browned. Cool on baking sheets for 2 minutes before removing.

Buttermilk Cookies

3½ cups flour
1 teaspoon salt
1 teaspoon baking soda
1 teaspoon baking powder
1 cup butter or margarine, softened
2 cups sugar
2 eggs
1 cup buttermilk
Milk
Colored sugar

In small bowl, blend flour, salt, baking soda, and baking powder. In large mixing bowl, cream together butter and sugar. Add eggs. Slowly mix in dry ingredients, alternating with buttermilk. Chill dough for at least 2 hours. Drop by teaspoonfuls onto greased cookie sheets. Dip bottom of glass into milk and press lightly on each cookie, flattening slightly. Sprinkle with colored sugar. Bake at 350° for 8 to 10 minutes.

Cocoa Nut Drop Cookies

1 cup sugar
¼ cup butter, softened
1 egg, beaten
½ cup milk
1½ cups flour
2 teaspoons baking powder
½ cup cocoa
1 cup nuts, chopped

Cream sugar and butter. Add egg and milk to sugar and butter mixture. In separate bowl, sift together flour, baking powder, and cocoa. Add to mixture. Add nuts and stir well. Drop with spoon onto greased cookie sheets. Bake at 375° for 15 minutes.

Cookies in a Jiffy

1 (9 ounce) yellow cake mix
⅔ cup quick-cooking oats
½ cup butter or margarine, melted
1 egg
½ cup M&M's or butterscotch chips

In mixing bowl, beat first four ingredients. Stir in M&M's or chips. Drop by tablespoonfuls 2 inches apart onto ungreased baking sheets. Bake at 350° for 10 to 12 minutes or until lightly browned. Immediately remove to wire racks to cool.
Makes 2 dozen.

Remember the true reason for the season: The greatest gift of Love ever given came in the form of a baby in a humble manger.

This is how God showed his love among us: He sent his one and only Son into the world that we might live through him.

1 JOHN 4:9

Cowboy Cookies

2 cups flour, sifted
1 teaspoon baking soda
½ teaspoon salt
½ teaspoon baking powder
1 cup shortening
1 cup sugar

1 cup brown sugar
2 eggs
2 cups rolled oats
1 teaspoon vanilla
1 cup semisweet chocolate chips

Sift together flour, baking soda, salt, and baking powder. Set aside. Blend shortening and sugars. Add eggs and beat until light. Add flour mixture and mix well. Add rolled oats, vanilla, and chocolate chips. Drop by teaspoonfuls onto greased cookie sheets. Bake at 350° for 15 minutes.

Cracker Jack Cookies

1 cup butter, softened
1 cup sugar
1 cup brown sugar
2 eggs
2 teaspoons vanilla
1½ cups flour
1 teaspoon baking powder
1 teaspoon baking soda
2 cups oats
1 cup flaked coconut
2 cups crispy rice cereal

Cream butter; add sugars, eggs, and vanilla. Cream well. Combine flour, baking powder, and baking soda; add to butter mixture. Mix well. By hand, stir in oats, coconut, and cereal. Drop by teaspoonfuls onto greased cookie sheets. Bake at 350° for 10 to 12 minutes or until nicely browned.

Delicious Cookies

1 cup nuts, chopped
1 cup flaked coconut
1 cup quick-cooking oats
1 cup crispy rice cereal
1 cup butter, softened
1 cup oil
1 cup brown sugar

1 cup sugar
2 eggs
3½ cups flour
1 teaspoon cream of tartar
1 teaspoon baking soda
½ teaspoon salt

Mix nuts, coconut, oats, and cereal; set aside. Cream together butter, oil, and sugars. Beat in eggs. Sift and add flour, cream of tartar, baking soda, and salt. Add first mixture. Drop by teaspoonfuls onto ungreased cookie sheets and flatten with fork. Bake at 350° for 8 minutes.

Ginger Cream Cookies

½ cup shortening
1 cup sugar
2 eggs
1 cup molasses
4 cups flour
1 teaspoon salt
2 teaspoons ginger
1 teaspoon ground cloves
1 teaspoon cinnamon
2 teaspoons baking soda
1 cup hot water

Cream shortening, sugar, and eggs. Add molasses. Sift together all dry ingredients, except baking soda. Dissolve baking soda in hot water; add alternately to dry ingredients. Chill dough thoroughly. Drop by teaspoonfuls 2 inches apart onto greased cookie sheets. Bake at 400° for 8 minutes. While still warm, ice with a thin white frosting of your choice.

Hazelnut Meringue Cookies

2 egg whites
½ cup sugar
⅛ teaspoon salt
½ teaspoon vanilla
½ teaspoon vinegar
1 cup hazelnuts

Line cookie sheets with either brown paper or parchment paper. Beat egg whites until soft peaks form. Gradually add sugar and salt; continue beating for 3 to 4 minutes until meringue is very stiff and sugar has dissolved. Beat in vanilla and vinegar. Fold in hazelnuts. Drop by spoonfuls in small mounds (about 1½ inches) on prepared cookie sheets. Bake at 300° for 30 minutes or until light brown. Turn off heat. Leave in oven until oven is cool or overnight to thoroughly dry. Lift off paper. Makes 2 dozen.

You've taken time to make beautiful cookies, so show off your gift in a nifty box. Cut one or more designs in the lid of a shoe box or other small box with a solid lid. Wrap the box with paper (foils work great), trimming flush with the cutout. Tape plastic wrap (clear or colored) over the cutout on the inside of the box. Let your home-baked gift peek through.

Holiday Fruit Drop Cookies

1 cup shortening
2 cups brown sugar, packed
2 eggs
½ cup sour milk or ⅔ cup buttermilk
3½ cups flour
1 teaspoon baking soda
1 teaspoon salt
1 cup nuts, chopped
2 cups candied cherries, cut into small pieces
2 cups dates, cut into small pieces (or 1 cup candied cherries and 1 cup dates, cut up)

Mix shortening, sugar, and eggs well. Stir in milk. Blend flour, baking soda, and salt; stir into shortening mixture. Add nuts, cherries, and dates. Chill for 1 hour. Heat oven to 400°. Drop dough by spoonfuls onto greased baking sheets or form into balls. Bake for 8 to 10 minutes. Makes 8 dozen.

Instant Pudding Cookies

½ cup margarine, softened
½ cup sugar
1 (3.4 ounce) package instant pudding
2 eggs, slightly beaten
1½ cups flour
½ teaspoon baking soda
¼ teaspoon salt

Cream margarine and sugar. Add pudding mix, eggs, flour, baking soda, and salt. Mix together well. Drop by teaspoonfuls onto ungreased baking sheets. Bake at 350° for 12 minutes or until lightly brown. Add nuts or frost if desired. Makes 3 dozen.

Lemon Snowflake Cookies

1 lemon cake mix with pudding
1 egg
2¼ cups frozen whipped topping, thawed
2 cups powdered sugar

Mix cake mix, egg, and whipped topping together. Beat with electric mixer on medium speed until well blended and sticky. Drop 1 teaspoon batter into powdered sugar and roll to coat. Place cookies on ungreased baking sheets. Bake at 350° for 8 to 10 minutes or until lightly browned.

Oatmeal Drop Cookies

2 cups flour, sifted
1½ cups sugar
1 teaspoon baking powder
½ teaspoon baking soda
½ teaspoon salt
1 teaspoon cinnamon
3 cups rolled oats
1 cup raisins
¾ to 1 cup semisweet chocolate chips (optional)
1 cup oil
2 eggs
½ cup milk

Sift together flour, sugar, baking powder, baking soda, salt, and cinnamon. Mix in oats, raisins, and, if desired, chocolate chips. Add in order oil, eggs, and milk. Mix until thoroughly blended. Drop by teaspoonfuls onto ungreased cookie sheets. Bake at 375° for 10 minutes. Makes about 6 dozen.

Orange Cranberry Drops

½ cup sugar
½ cup brown sugar, packed
¼ cup butter, softened
1 egg
3 tablespoons orange juice
½ teaspoon orange extract
1 teaspoon orange zest
1½ cups flour
½ teaspoon baking powder
¼ teaspoon baking soda
¼ teaspoon salt
1 cup dried cranberries

Cream together sugars and butter. Stir in egg, orange juice, orange extract, and orange zest. Sift together flour, baking powder, baking soda, and salt. Stir dry ingredients into orange mixture. Fold in dried cranberries. Drop by heaping teaspoonfuls 2 inches apart onto greased cookie sheets. Bake at 375° for 10 to 12 minutes or until edges begin to brown. Cool on baking sheets or remove to cool on wire racks.

Dear heavenly Father, may the love that shines from my heart be an example to others, as I want them to see You through me. Help me to use my love every day in small ways, for it's often the simple acts of love that hold the most profound meaning and have the greatest effect upon hearts.

Pumpkin Butterscotch Cookies

1½ cups pumpkin
½ cup margarine
1 cup sugar
½ teaspoon salt
1 teaspoon vanilla
1 cup walnuts, chopped
1 egg
2 cups flour
1 teaspoon salt
1 teaspoon baking powder
1 teaspoon cinnamon
1 package butterscotch chips

Mix all ingredients in order given; drop by spoonfuls onto greased cookie sheets.
Bake at 375° for 12 to 14 minutes. Makes 4 dozen.

VARIATIONS:

Raisins, pecans, or flaked coconut may be substituted for butterscotch chips.
Also, 3 ripe bananas may be substituted for pumpkin.

Quick 'n' Easy
Peanut Butter Cookies

1 cup peanut butter (smooth or crunchy)
1 egg
1 cup sugar

Spray two cookie sheets with vegetable cooking spray. Mix ingredients together
and drop by spoonfuls onto cookie sheets. Bake at 350° for 8 to 12 minutes.
Do not brown cookies on top as bottoms will burn. Makes 3 dozen.

Stir-and-Drop Sugar Cookies

2 eggs
⅔ cup vegetable oil
2 teaspoons vanilla
1 teaspoon lemon zest
¾ cup sugar
2 teaspoons baking powder
2 cups flour
½ teaspoon salt
Vegetable oil
Sugar

Beat eggs and stir in oil, vanilla, and lemon zest. Blend in sugar and beat until thick. Add remaining ingredients. Drop 2 inches apart onto ungreased cookie sheets. Flatten with glass dipped in oil and sugar. Bake at 400° for 8 to 10 minutes.

When making drop cookies, make a double batch. Form the extra dough into cookie-sized balls and freeze them on a cookie sheet. When frozen, put the dough balls into labeled plastic bags and store in the freezer. Later, you can remove just the number of cookies you need to bake. No need for thawing. Now you can have a variety of cookies ready to bake for unexpected guests or for quick, tasty gifts.

Yummy Chocolate Cookies

May you have. . .the heart of Christmas, which is Love.
AVA V. HENDRICKS

Chewy Chocolate Cookies

1 chocolate cake mix
2 eggs
1 cup Miracle Whip
1 cup semisweet chocolate chips
½ cup walnuts, chopped (optional)

Mix cake mix, eggs, and Miracle Whip in large bowl with electric mixer on medium speed.
Stir in remaining ingredients. Drop by rounded teaspoonfuls onto greased cookie sheets.
Bake at 350° for 10 to 12 minutes or until edges are lightly browned.
Makes 4 dozen.

Chocolate Almond Tea Cakes

¾ cup margarine or butter, softened
⅓ cup powdered sugar
1 cup flour
½ cup instant cocoa mix
½ cup toasted almonds, diced
Powdered sugar

Combine margarine and ⅓ cup powdered sugar. Stir in flour, cocoa mix, and almonds. (If dough is too soft to shape, refrigerate until firm.) Heat oven to 325°. Shape dough into 1-inch balls and place on ungreased cookie sheets. Bake about 20 minutes or until set. Dip tops in powdered sugar while still warm. Let cool and dip again. Makes 4 dozen.

Chocolate Caramel Cookies

2½ cups flour
1 teaspoon baking soda
½ teaspoon baking powder
1 teaspoon salt
1 cup butter, softened
1 cup sugar
½ cup brown sugar, packed
2 eggs
1 cup semisweet chocolate chips
18 caramels, unwrapped and chopped into bits
1 cup nuts (pecans or walnuts), coarsely chopped

Whisk together flour, baking soda, baking powder, and salt; set aside. Using electric mixer, cream together butter and sugars. Beat in eggs one at a time. Gradually add flour mixture, beating after each addition. Stir in chocolate chips, caramels, and nuts until just mixed. Drop by rounded tablespoonfuls about 2 inches apart onto nonstick baking sheets. Bake at 375° for 10 to 12 minutes or until lightly golden. Cool cookies on baking sheets until firm.

Chocolate Chip Banana Cookies

2½ cups flour
2 teaspoons baking powder
½ teaspoon salt
¼ teaspoon baking soda
⅔ cup butter, softened
1 cup sugar
2 eggs
1 teaspoon vanilla
1 cup ripe bananas, mashed
2 cups semisweet chocolate chips

Sift together flour, baking powder, salt, and baking soda; set aside. Cream butter and sugar until light and fluffy. Beat in eggs one at a time, then vanilla. Mix in bananas. Add flour mixture, stirring until just combined. Stir in chocolate chips. Drop by spoonfuls onto greased cookie sheets. Bake at 400° for 12 to 15 minutes.

Chocolate Chip Coconut Cookies

⅓ cup shortening
⅓ cup butter, softened
½ cup sugar
½ cup brown sugar
1 egg
1 teaspoon vanilla

1½ cups flour
½ teaspoon baking soda
½ teaspoon salt
1 cup semisweet chocolate chips
¼ package flaked coconut
1 to 2 cups oats

Mix shortening, butter, sugars, egg, and vanilla. Blend in flour, baking soda, and salt.
Mix in chocolate chips, coconut, and oats. Drop by rounded teaspoonfuls 2 inches
apart onto ungreased baking sheets. Bake at 375° for 8 to 10 minutes.
Cool slightly before removing from baking sheet.

Chocolate Chip Cookie Balls

1 devil's food cake mix
1 egg
¾ cup vegetable oil
1½ cups semisweet chocolate chips
½ cup pecans, chopped

Mix all ingredients together. Roll into 1-inch balls. Place on ungreased cookie sheets.
Bake at 350° for 5 to 7 minutes. Cool on rack. Store in airtight container.
Makes about 2 dozen.

Host a cookie-baking party with family and friends. Invite each person to bring a few ingredients, then pool them together and bake all afternoon. Allow the kids to join in when you're ready to decorate the cutouts.

Chocolate Chip Treasure Cookies

1 (14 ounce) can sweetened condensed milk
½ cup butter, softened
1½ cups graham cracker crumbs
½ cup flour
2 teaspoons baking powder
1½ cups flaked coconut
2 cups mini semisweet chocolate chips
1 cup pecans, chopped
1 cup raisins

Beat condensed milk and butter. Add graham cracker crumbs, flour, and baking powder. Mix well. Add remaining ingredients. Drop by spoonfuls onto greased cookie sheets. Bake at 375° for 9 to 10 minutes until lightly brown. Makes 4 dozen or more, depending on size.

Chocolate Crinkles

1 cup cocoa
2 cups sugar
2 teaspoons vanilla
½ teaspoon salt
½ cup vegetable oil
4 eggs
2 cups flour
2 teaspoons baking powder
Powdered sugar (optional)

Combine all ingredients except powdered sugar, mixing well. Refrigerate overnight.
Form balls and roll in powdered sugar. Bake at 350° for 10 to 12 minutes.
Sprinkle with powdered sugar after baking if desired.

Chocolate Peppermint Creams

3 cups flour
1¼ teaspoons baking soda
½ teaspoon salt
¾ cup butter

1½ cups brown sugar, packed
2 tablespoons water
2 cups semisweet chocolate chips
2 eggs

Sift together flour, baking soda, and salt. In large saucepan over low heat, melt butter with brown sugar and water. Add chocolate chips and stir until melted. Remove from heat; cool slightly. Beat in eggs. Add flour mixture and mix well. Drop by teaspoonfuls onto greased cookie sheets. Bake at 350° for 8 to 10 minutes. Cool. Pair cookies together with 1 teaspoon filling. Makes about 3 dozen filled.

PEPPERMINT FILLING:

3 cups powdered sugar
⅓ cup butter, softened
¼ teaspoon peppermint extract

¼ cup milk
5 drops green food coloring

Blend ingredients together with mixer in small bowl.
Note: Chocolate chips, butter, and water may be heated in the microwave for 2 minutes on high or until chocolate melts (microwaves may vary). Add brown sugar, mixing well.

For vibrant colors in your cookies, use paste rather than liquid colors for decorating dough and icing.

Chocolate Snowballs

1¼ cups butter, softened
⅔ cup sugar
1 teaspoon vanilla
2 cups flour
⅛ teaspoon salt
½ cup cocoa
2 cups pecans, chopped
½ cup powdered sugar

In medium bowl, cream butter and sugar until light and fluffy. Stir in vanilla. Sift together flour, salt, and cocoa; stir into creamed mixture. Mix in pecans until well blended. Cover and chill for at least 2 hours. Preheat oven to 350°. Roll chilled dough into 1-inch balls. Place about 2 inches apart on ungreased cookie sheets. Bake for 20 minutes in preheated oven. Roll in powdered sugar when cooled.

Chocolate Striped Cookies

½ cup butter, softened
½ cup shortening
1 cup sugar
½ teaspoon baking soda
⅛ teaspoon salt
1 egg
2 tablespoons milk

1 teaspoon vanilla
3 cups flour
⅓ cup semisweet chocolate chips,
   melted and cooled
½ cup nuts, finely chopped
½ cup mini semisweet chocolate
   chips
¼ teaspoon almond extract

Beat butter and shortening on medium to high speed for 30 seconds. Add sugar, baking soda, and salt; beat until combined. Beat in egg, milk, and vanilla. Beat in as much of the flour as you can with the mixer, then stir in remaining flour by hand. Divide dough in half. Knead melted chocolate and nuts into half of dough. Knead mini chocolate chips and almond extract into other half of dough. Divide each portion of dough in half. Line bottom and sides of 9 x 5 x 3-inch loaf pan with plastic wrap. Press half of chocolate dough evenly in pan. Layer with half of almond, remaining chocolate, then remaining almond dough to form four even, flat layers. Invert pan to remove dough and peel off plastic wrap. Cut dough crosswise into ¼-inch-thick slices. Place cookies 2 inches apart on ungreased cookie sheets. Bake at 375° for about 10 minutes.

Chocolate Striped Cookie dough can be made and frozen in a plastic freezer bag up to a month in advance.

Chocolate Toffee Cookies

2¼ cups flour
1 teaspoon baking soda
1 cup butter, softened
¼ cup sugar
¾ cup brown sugar
1 teaspoon vanilla
1 (3.4 ounce) package instant vanilla pudding
2 eggs
2 cups semisweet chocolate chips
½ package toffee bits

Sift together flour and baking soda. In separate bowl, mix butter, sugars, vanilla, and pudding mix. Mix until smooth. Beat in eggs. Slowly add flour mixture. Stir in chocolate chips and toffee bits. Bake at 375° for 8 to 10 minutes.

Chunky Chocolate Cookies

1 (4 ounce) bar sweet chocolate
½ cup butter
½ cup sugar
¼ cup brown sugar
1 egg
1 teaspoon vanilla
1 cup flour
½ teaspoon baking soda
½ teaspoon salt
½ cup nuts, coarsely chopped

Chop chocolate bar into bite-sized pieces; set aside. Cream butter until soft. Add sugars, egg, and vanilla; beat until light and fluffy. Add flour, baking soda, and salt. Stir in chocolate pieces and nuts. Drop by teaspoonfuls 2 inches apart onto ungreased cookie sheets. Bake at 375° for 8 to 10 minutes or until lightly browned.

Crispy Chocolate Chip Cookies

1 cup butter, softened
1 cup sugar
1 cup brown sugar
2 eggs
1 teaspoon vanilla
1 teaspoon salt
1 teaspoon baking soda
2½ cups flour
1½ cups oats
1½ cups crispy rice cereal
2 cups semisweet chocolate chips

Cream together butter and sugars. Beat in eggs and vanilla. In separate bowl, combine salt, baking soda, and flour. Stir into creamed mixture. Stir in oats and cereal, then chocolate chips. Drop by spoonfuls onto ungreased cookie sheets and bake at 350° for 10 minutes.

Oatmeal Chocolate Chip Cookies

1½ cups flour
2½ cups oats
1 teaspoon salt
¾ cup brown sugar
¾ cup sugar
1 cup shortening
2 eggs
1 teaspoon vanilla
1 teaspoon baking soda
1 cup semisweet chocolate chips
½ cup nuts, chopped

Mix together flour, oats, and salt. Cream together sugars and shortening; add eggs, vanilla, and baking soda dissolved in hot water. Stir in flour mixture, then chocolate chips and nuts. Drop by spoonfuls onto greased cookie sheets. Bake at 400° until light brown.

Pudding 'n' Chocolate Chip Cookies

2 packages vanilla pudding (instant or regular)
2 cups all-purpose baking mix
½ cup vegetable oil or applesauce
2 eggs
6 tablespoons milk
1 cup semisweet chocolate chips

Mix ingredients in order given. Drop by teaspoonfuls onto ungreased cookie sheets.
Bake at 350° for 8 to 10 minutes.

Rocky Road Cookies

½ cup butter
1 cup semisweet chocolate
   chips, divided
1 cup sugar
2 eggs
½ teaspoon vanilla

1½ cups flour
½ teaspoon baking powder
¼ teaspoon salt
1 cup nuts, chopped
48 mini marshmallows

Melt butter and ½ cup chocolate chips in small saucepan, stirring frequently. Remove from heat and set aside to cool. In medium bowl, stir together melted chocolate mixture with sugar, eggs, and vanilla. In separate bowl, sift together flour, baking powder, and salt; stir into chocolate mixture. Finally, stir in nuts and remaining chocolate chips. Drop dough by rounded teaspoonfuls onto ungreased cookie sheets. Press miniature marshmallow into center of each cookie. Bake at 400° for 7 to 8 minutes. Remove from cookie sheets immediately to cool on wire racks.

Secret Kiss Cookies

1 cup butter, softened
½ cup sugar
1 teaspoon vanilla
1¾ cups flour
1 cup walnuts, finely chopped
1 (6 ounce) bag chocolate kiss candies
Powdered sugar

Beat butter, sugar, and vanilla until light and fluffy. Add flour and walnuts; mix well. Chill dough for 1 to 2 hours. Remove wrappers from chocolate kisses. Shape about 1 tablespoon dough around each chocolate kiss. Roll to make ball. (Be sure to cover chocolate completely.) Bake at 375° for 10 to 12 minutes. While still slightly warm, roll in powdered sugar.

Triple Chocolate Chip Cookies

1 chocolate cake mix
1 (4-serving size) package instant chocolate pudding
1 cup sour cream
1 cup semisweet chocolate chips
2 large eggs

Combine all five ingredients in bowl. Stir until moistened and no big lumps remain.
Drop by rounded spoonfuls about 2 inches apart onto greased cookie sheets.
Bake at 350° for 16 to 18 minutes. Let stand for 2 minutes. Cool completely.

Turtle Cookies

½ cup brown sugar, packed
½ cup margarine or butter,
  softened
2 tablespoons water
1 teaspoon vanilla

1½ cups flour
⅛ teaspoon salt
Pecan halves
8 caramels, each cut into fourths

Combine brown sugar, margarine, water, and vanilla. Stir in flour and salt until dough holds together. (Add 1 to 2 teaspoons water if dough is dry.) Heat oven to 350°. Group together 3 to 5 pecan halves for each cookie on ungreased cookie sheets. Shape dough by teaspoonfuls around caramel pieces; press firmly onto center of each group of nuts.

Bake until set, but do not brown, for 12 to 15 minutes.

Cool, then dip tops of cookies into chocolate glaze. Makes 2½ dozen.

CHOCOLATE GLAZE:

1 cup powdered sugar
1 tablespoon water

1 ounce unsweetened chocolate
1 teaspoon vanilla

Melt unsweetened chocolate, then let cool. In separate bowl, beat powdered sugar, water, unsweetened chocolate, and vanilla until smooth. Stir in water, 1 teaspoon at a time, until glaze reaches desired consistency.

Sweet 'n' Simple No-Bake Cookies

The joy of brightening other lives, bearing each other's burdens, easing others' loads, and supplanting empty hearts and lives with generous gifts becomes for us the magic of Christmas.
W. C. JONES

Cherry Surprises

½ cup butter, softened
1¾ cups powdered sugar
1 teaspoon orange juice
1½ cups flaked coconut
1 (10 ounce) jar maraschino cherries, drained

In medium bowl, cream together butter, powdered sugar, and orange juice; mix in coconut. Wrap coconut mixture around each cherry to cover completely. Store in refrigerator in tightly covered container until ready to serve.

Coconut Bonbons

¼ cup butter, softened
1 pound powdered sugar
1 cup sweetened condensed milk
2 cups flaked coconut
9 (1 ounce) squares semisweet chocolate
2 tablespoons shortening

In medium bowl, combine butter, powdered sugar, and sweetened condensed milk. Stir in coconut; mix well. Roll mixture into 1-inch balls. Refrigerate until set, about 1 hour. Melt chocolate and shortening over double boiler, stirring occasionally until melted and smooth. Remove from heat and stir. Use toothpicks to hold balls while dipping in chocolate. Set on waxed paper to dry.

Cookie Dough Balls

1 cup butter, softened
1½ cups brown sugar, packed
2 teaspoons vanilla
½ teaspoon salt
2 cups flour
1 tablespoon water
1 cup mini semisweet chocolate chips

Cream butter and brown sugar. Stir in remaining ingredients; mix well by hand. Roll into bite-sized balls. Freeze until firm, about 30 minutes. Store in resealable plastic bag in freezer. Thaw at room temperature 5 minutes before serving. Makes 4 dozen.

Crispy Cookies

½ cup sugar
½ cup light corn syrup
1 cup peanut butter
2 cups crispy rice cereal

Bring sugar and syrup to a full boil. Remove from heat. Add peanut butter and cereal.
Drop by teaspoonfuls onto waxed paper.

Easy 5-in-1 No-Bake Cookies

BASE:
½ cup peanut butter
½ cup honey or light corn syrup
¼ cup orange juice concentrate
1½ cups nonfat dry milk

Mix above ingredients thoroughly. Now choose one of the following five steps:

OATMEAL RAISIN:
2 cups rolled oats
1½ cups raisins

Mix into base. Shape into bite-sized balls, then flatten.

CRISPY BALLS:
4 cups crispy rice cereal

Mix into base. Shape into bite-sized balls.
(cont.)

84

Raisin Clusters:
¼ cup cocoa
4 cups raisins

Mix into base. Form into bite-sized balls.

Cocoa Balls:
¼ cup cocoa
2 cups rolled oats
¼ cup peanuts, chopped
1 teaspoon vanilla

Mix into base. Shape into bite-sized balls.

Grahamies:
¼ cup raisins
Graham crackers

Mix raisins into base. Spread mixture between graham crackers.

Granola Bites

1 cup powdered sugar
1 cup creamy peanut butter
⅓ cup milk
1 teaspoon vanilla
1½ cups oats
1 cup granola cereal
1¾ cups peanut butter and milk chocolate chips

Line two cookie sheets with waxed paper. In large bowl, combine powdered sugar, peanut butter, milk, and vanilla; mix well. Stir in oats, cereal, and chips. Mix until cereal is evenly coated. Roll mixture into 1-inch balls and place on prepared cookie sheets.
Let stand until firm. Store in airtight container.

No-Bake Fudge Cookies

½ cup butter or margarine, cut into pieces
½ cup milk
2 cups sugar
⅓ cup cocoa
1 teaspoon salt
1 teaspoon vanilla
4 cups quick-cooking oats

Line tray or cookie sheet with waxed paper. Combine butter and milk in large microwave-safe bowl. Microwave on high for 1 minute or until butter is melted. Stir in sugar and cocoa until mixed. Microwave on high for 1½ minutes; stir. Microwave on high for an additional 1½ to 3 minutes or until sugar is completely dissolved. Stir in salt, vanilla, and oats. Drop by spoonfuls onto prepared tray or cookie sheet. Flatten slightly and let stand until firm. Makes 3 dozen.

No-Bake Peanut Oatmeal Drops

1 cup sugar
¼ cup butter
⅓ cup evaporated milk
1 cup peanut butter
½ teaspoon vanilla
1 cup rolled oats
½ cup peanuts

Bring sugar, butter, and milk to a rolling boil. Boil for 3 minutes, stirring frequently.
Remove from heat and stir in peanut butter, vanilla, rolled oats, and peanuts.
Drop by teaspoonfuls onto waxed paper. Let stand until set.

No-Bake Pudding Cookies

2 cups sugar
¾ cup butter
6 ounces evaporated milk
1 (3.4 ounce) package butterscotch instant pudding
3½ cups quick-cooking oats

In medium saucepan, combine sugar, butter, and evaporated milk. Bring to a boil and continue boiling for 1 minute. Remove from heat and stir in pudding mix and oats. Spoon mixture onto sheet of waxed paper. Allow to cool until firm.

A pretty but simple Christmas tree decoration is a cookie cutter tied with festive holiday ribbon. Purchase a few dozen cookie cutters and have a cookie-themed Christmas tree this year!

Peanut Butter Cornflake Cookies

1 cup sugar
1 cup light corn syrup
1½ cups peanut butter
1 teaspoon vanilla
8 cups cornflakes

Combine sugar and syrup in saucepan; heat to a full boil. Remove from heat and add peanut butter and vanilla. Beat until smooth. Pour mixture over cornflakes and stir until flakes are completely coated. Drop by teaspoonfuls onto waxed paper. Makes 3 dozen.

Snookie Cookies

½ cup walnuts, broken
½ cup dates
½ pound colored marshmallows, cut in pieces
½ cup unsweetened condensed milk
¼ cup boiling water
2½ cups graham cracker crumbs

Combine first four ingredients and pour boiling water over mixture. Stir in graham cracker crumbs. Shape into roll about 2 inches thick. Let stand overnight. Cut into slices.

Snowmen Cookies

1 (16 ounce) package Nutter Butter cookies
1¼ pounds white candy coating, melted
Licorice strings
Mini semisweet chocolate chips
M&M's mini baking bits
Pretzel sticks, halved
Orange and red frosting

Using tongs, dip cookies into candy coating. Shake off excess. Place on waxed paper. Using pieces of licorice, create hat on upper portion of cookie. Place two chocolate chips for eyes. Place baking bits down lower half of cookie for buttons. For arms, dip ends of pretzel stick halves into coating; attach one to each side. Let stand until hardened. Pipe nose with orange frosting. Pipe scarf at indented point with red frosting.

Stovetop Cookies

1 cup flaked coconut
1 cup sugar
2 large eggs, beaten
1 cup dates, chopped
1 tablespoon butter
2 cups crispy rice cereal
1 cup pecans, chopped
1 teaspoon vanilla

Sprinkle coconut evenly onto 15 x 10 x 1-inch baking pan lined with waxed paper. Set aside. In large saucepan, combine sugar and eggs; stir well. Add dates and butter. Cook over low heat, stirring constantly, for 8 minutes or until mixture is thick and bubbly. Remove from heat and stir in cereal, pecans, and vanilla; mix well. Spread cereal mixture evenly into prepared pan. Let stand for 15 minutes. Roll mixture into 15-inch log. Allow to cool completely. Cut into ½ -inch-thick slices. Store in airtight container.

Swedish No-Bake Chocolate Balls

1½ cups margarine, softened
2 cups sugar
3 tablespoons dark coffee (liquid)
3 tablespoons cocoa
3 teaspoons vanilla
5 cups quick-cooking oats
Flaked coconut and colored sprinkles

Mix first six ingredients and form into ¾-inch balls.
Dip in coconut and colored sprinkles. Refrigerate.

Traditional No-Bake Cookies

½ cup butter or margarine
½ cup milk
2 cups sugar
½ cup cocoa
1 cup peanut butter
1 teaspoon vanilla
3 cups oats

Combine butter, milk, sugar, and cocoa in large saucepan. Bring to a rolling boil. Boil for 3 minutes (do not overboil); remove from heat, then add peanut butter, vanilla, and oats. Drop by heaping teaspoonfuls onto sheet of waxed paper. Let cool until firm. Store in airtight container in cool, dry place.

Festive Rolled, Shaped & Pressed Cookies

Christmas may be a day of feasting, or of prayer, but always it will be a day of remembrance—a day in which we think of everything we have ever loved.
AUGUSTA E. RUNDEL

Buried Cherry Cookies

1 cup sugar
½ cup margarine
1 egg
1½ teaspoons vanilla
1½ cups flour
⅓ cup cocoa

¼ teaspoon baking powder
¼ teaspoon baking soda
¼ teaspoon salt
1 (6 ounce) jar maraschino cherries,
    drained, juice reserved

Cream sugar and margarine. Beat in egg and vanilla. Add flour, cocoa, baking powder, baking soda, and salt; mix. Shape dough into 1-inch balls. Press down center with thumb. Insert cherry and cover with frosting. Bake at 350° for 8 to 10 minutes.

FROSTING:
½ cup semisweet chocolate chips
¼ cup sweetened condensed milk
2 teaspoons cherry juice

Melt together all frosting ingredients.

Butterhorn Cookies

1 cup butter   1 egg yolk
2½ cups flour   ¾ cup sour cream

Work butter into flour with fingers. Add egg yolk and sour cream, blending well. Shape into ball, sprinkle with flour, and wrap with waxed paper. Chill for several hours or days (the longer the better). Divide chilled dough into four pieces and, with rolling pin, roll one at a time into a circle as if making a piecrust. Roll out to ⅛-inch thickness. Sprinkle with cinnamon mixture and cut into pieces as if cutting a pie. (Be sure to use lots of cinnamon mix.) Roll each piece as if making a crescent roll. Set on greased cookie sheet. Bake at 350° for 20 to 30 minutes or until golden brown. Remove quickly from cookie sheet and let cool on breadboard or any cold surface.

CINNAMON MIX:
¾ cup sugar
1 teaspoon cinnamon
¾ cup almonds, chopped

Mix sugar, cinnamon, and almonds together.

Prepare all your Butterhorn Cookies first, before you start baking.

Candy Cane Twisties

½ cup butter, softened
½ cup shortening
1 cup sugar
¼ cup powdered sugar
½ cup milk
1 egg

1 teaspoon peppermint extract
1 teaspoon vanilla
3½ cups flour
¼ teaspoon salt
Green and red food coloring

Cream butter, shortening, and sugars. Blend in milk, egg, peppermint, and vanilla. Gradually add flour and salt. Set aside half of dough. Divide remaining dough in half, adding green food coloring to one portion and red to the other. Wrap dough separately in plastic wrap. Refrigerate for 1 hour or until easy to handle. Roll ½ teaspoonful of each color of dough into 3-inch ropes. Place each green rope next to a white rope; press together gently and twist. Repeat with red ropes and remaining white ropes. Place 2 inches apart on ungreased baking sheets. Curve one end, forming a cane. Bake at 350° for 11 to 13 minutes or until set. Cool for 2 minutes; carefully remove to wire racks.

The best gift you can give this year is the gift of your love. Be sure to tell your loved ones how much you care. This is a great way to warm hearts on cold winter days—(especially if you're out of hot chocolate)!

Above all, love each other deeply.
1 PETER 4:8

Cherry Christmas Cookies

1 cup butter, softened
¾ cup brown sugar
½ teaspoon vanilla
⅛ teaspoon salt
2½ cups flour
1 cup almonds, sliced
½ cup red cherries, whole
½ cup green cherries, whole

Cream butter; add sugar and then vanilla, salt, and flour. Finally, add almonds and cherries and form into rolls. Leave in refrigerator overnight.
Slice thin with sharp knife and bake on greased baking sheets at 375° for 10 minutes.

Christmas Log Cookies

¾ cup shortening
¼ cup butter, softened
1 cup powdered sugar
1¼ cups flour
½ teaspoon salt
2 teaspoons vanilla
1 cup oats
Flaked coconut or nuts, chopped

Cream shortening, butter, and sugar until fluffy. Add flour, salt, vanilla, and oats and mix well. Lay sheet of foil on counter; sprinkle coconut or nuts on top of foil. Shape dough into log and place on foil. Pat nuts or coconut all around dough. Wrap dough and seal tightly. Refrigerate overnight or for up to a week. Slice and place on ungreased cookie sheets. Bake at 400° for 7 to 8 minutes.

When slicing logs of refrigerated cookie dough, roll the dough every other cut so the bottom of the log doesn't flatten and so each cookie will be perfectly round.

Cinnamon Twisties

2 cups sugar
2 cups walnuts, ground
1 tablespoon cinnamon
1 cup butter, softened
1 (8 ounce) package cream cheese, softened
2½ cups flour
1 egg, beaten

Mix together sugar, walnuts, and cinnamon; set aside. In another bowl, cream butter and
cream cheese. Gradually add flour. If dough is too soft, add a little more flour.
Roll out dough to ½-inch thickness and brush with beaten egg. Cover with cinnamon
mixture. Cut into 1½-inch strips and twist. Place on ungreased cookie sheets.
Bake at 400° for 8 to 10 minutes.

Gingersnaps

2¼ cups flour
2 teaspoons baking soda
1 teaspoon cinnamon
1 teaspoon ground ginger
½ teaspoon ground cloves
¼ teaspoon salt
1 cup light brown sugar, packed
¾ cup shortening
¼ cup molasses
1 egg

Sift together first six ingredients and set aside. Combine remaining ingredients and beat well. Add dry ingredients to beaten mixture. Form into 1-inch balls. Roll in powdered sugar if desired. Place balls 2 inches apart on ungreased cookie sheets. Bake for approximately 10 minutes. Makes about 4 dozen.

Jam Thumbprint Cookies

½ cup butter, softened
⅓ cup sugar
1 egg yolk
1 teaspoon vanilla
1⅓ cups flour
¼ teaspoon salt
Jam or preserves, any flavor
Nuts, finely chopped

In large mixing bowl, cream butter until light. Add sugar and beat until fluffy, then beat in egg yolk and vanilla. Gradually mix in flour and salt. Dough will be very firm. Shape dough into 1-inch balls and place on greased cookie sheets. With thumb, press indentation into center of each cookie. Bake at 350° for 7 to 9 minutes or until firm. Remove from oven and fill each cookie with about ½ teaspoon jam, then sprinkle with chopped nuts. Return cookies to oven and bake for 6 to 8 minutes or until edges of cookies are light golden brown. Let cookies cool on baking sheets for 2 to 3 minutes before removing to cool on wire racks.

Lemon Snowballs

1 cup shortening
1⅓ cups sugar
4 teaspoons lemon zest
2 eggs
6 tablespoons lemon juice
2 tablespoons water

3½ cups flour
½ teaspoon baking soda
1 teaspoon salt
½ teaspoon cream of tartar
½ cup nuts, finely chopped
Powdered sugar

Thoroughly mix first four ingredients. Stir in lemon juice and water. Sift together remaining ingredients and add nuts; stir into lemon mixture. Form into walnut-sized balls. Place about 1 inch apart on ungreased baking sheets. Bake at 350° for about 10 minutes. Remove from baking sheets and roll in powdered sugar.

Melting Moments Cookies

1 scant cup flour
½ cup cornstarch
½ cup powdered sugar
¾ cup margarine, softened
1 teaspoon vanilla

Sift together flour, cornstarch, and powdered sugar. Add margarine and vanilla.
Stir all together. Form into bite-sized balls. Flatten balls if desired.
Bake at 370° for 10 to 12 minutes.

Peanut Butter Cookies

1½ cups butter, softened
1 cup sugar
1¼ cups peanut butter (smooth or chunky)
1 egg
½ teaspoon vanilla
½ teaspoon baking soda
1½ cups flour

Cream butter and sugar. Beat in peanut butter, egg, and vanilla. Mix in baking soda and flour. Roll dough into 1-inch balls and place about 2 inches apart on lightly greased cookie sheets. Press flat with palm of hand or flatten by crisscrossing with tines of fork. Bake at 350° for 10 to 12 minutes or until edges begin to brown.

Pecan Sandies

1 cup butter or margarine, softened
⅓ cup sugar
2 teaspoons water
2 teaspoons vanilla
1 cup flour
1 cup pecans, chopped
Powdered sugar

Cream butter and sugar; add water and vanilla; mix well. Add flour and pecans. Chill for 3 to 4 hours. Shape into balls or fingers. Bake at 325° for 20 minutes. Cool and roll in powdered sugar. Makes up to 5 dozen.

Russian Tea Cakes

1 cup butter, softened
½ cup powdered sugar
1 teaspoon vanilla
2½ cups flour
¼ teaspoon salt
¾ cup pecans or walnuts, finely chopped
Powdered sugar

Cream together butter, sugar, and vanilla. Gradually mix in flour, salt, and nuts. Shape into 1-inch balls and place on greased cookie sheets. Bake at 400° for 15 to 18 minutes. Roll hot balls in powdered sugar. Let cool, then roll in sugar again.

Snickerdoodle Cookies

1 cup shortening (or ½ cup
    shortening and ½ cup
    butter, softened)
1½ cups sugar
2 eggs

1 teaspoon baking soda
¼ teaspoon salt
2¾ cups flour
2 teaspoons cream of tartar

Mix shortening, sugar, and eggs. Add remaining ingredients. Roll into balls about 1 inch thick. Roll balls in coating mixture. Place balls 2 inches apart on ungreased cookie sheets. Bake at 350° for 8 to 10 minutes.

COATING:
2 tablespoons sugar
2 teaspoons cinnamon

Mix together sugar and cinnamon.

Do not overbake. Snickerdoodle Cookies will not look like they are done at the end of 8 to 10 minutes. They will be very soft but will harden as they cool.

Spritz

1½ cups butter
1 cup sugar
1 egg
1 teaspoon vanilla
1 teaspoon almond extract
1 teaspoon baking powder

¼ teaspoon salt
4 cups sifted flour
Decorating sugars
Cherries, chopped
Nuts, chopped

Cream butter until very soft. Work in sugar, then egg, vanilla, and almond extract. Sift together baking powder, flour, and salt; gradually add to butter mixture. Form cookies with cookie press on ungreased cookie sheets. Decorate with decorating sugars, chopped cherries, and/or nuts. Bake at 400° for 8 to 10 minutes.

Refrigerate ungreased cookie sheets until ready to use.

Holiday Best Brownies & Bars

Love came down at Christmas,
Love all lovely, Love Divine;
Love was born at Christmas;
Star and angels gave the sign.
CHRISTINA ROSSETTI

Brownies

1 cup sugar
½ cup butter, softened
2 eggs
½ cup milk
⅔ cup flour

½ teaspoon baking powder
1 cup nut meats
2 squares unsweetened chocolate, melted
1 teaspoon vanilla

Mix ingredients in order given. Pour into greased 9 x 13-inch baking pan. Bake at 350°
for 25 minutes. Cool before icing.

ICING:

1 cup brown sugar
1½ tablespoons butter
Pinch salt
¼ cup milk

1½ cups powdered sugar
1 teaspoon vanilla
2 tablespoons cocoa

Combine brown sugar, butter, salt, and milk. Bring to a boil and cook for 3 minutes. Cool to
lukewarm. Add powdered sugar, vanilla, and cocoa. Beat until smooth and spreadable.

A simple but always appreciated gift is a treat from your kitchen! Surprise neighbors and coworkers with plates of your "famous" cutouts. Decorate with pretty ribbon and attach a Christmassy cookie cutter along with your recipe. For a personal touch, add a heartfelt holiday sentiment or a favorite Bible verse.

Caramel Brownies

2 cups sugar
¾ cup cocoa
1 cup vegetable oil
4 eggs
¼ cup milk
1½ cups flour
1 teaspoon salt

1 teaspoon baking powder
1 cup semisweet chocolate
  chips
1 cup walnuts, chopped and
  divided
1 (14 ounce) package caramels
1 (14 ounce) can sweetened condensed
  milk

In mixing bowl, combine sugar, cocoa, oil, eggs, and milk. In separate bowl, combine flour, salt, and baking powder; add to egg mixture and mix well. Fold in chocolate chips and ½ cup walnuts. Spoon two-thirds of batter into greased 9 x 13-inch baking pan. Bake at 350° for 12 minutes. Meanwhile, in saucepan over low heat, heat caramels and sweetened condensed milk until caramels are melted. Pour over baked brownie layer. Sprinkle with remaining walnuts. Drop remaining batter by teaspoonfuls over caramel layer; carefully swirl brownie batter with knife. Bake 35 to 40 minutes longer or until toothpick inserted near center comes out with moist crumbs. Cool.

Cinnamon Coffee Bars

¼ cup shortening
1 cup brown sugar, packed
1 egg
½ cup hot coffee
1½ cups flour
1 teaspoon baking powder

¼ teaspoon baking soda
¼ teaspoon salt
1 teaspoon cinnamon
½ cup raisins
¼ cup nuts, chopped

Cream together shortening, brown sugar, and egg. Stir in hot coffee. Sift together flour, baking powder, baking soda, salt, and cinnamon. Add to creamed mixture. Blend in raisins and nuts. Spread in greased 9 x 13-inch baking pan. Bake at 350° for 18 to 20 minutes. Glaze while still hot. Cool and cut. Makes about 2 dozen bars.

GLAZE:
1 cup powdered sugar
1 teaspoon vanilla
1½ tablespoons milk

Mix all glaze ingredients.

Cream Cheese Brownies

1 brownie mix (family size)
1 (8 ounce) package cream cheese, softened
⅓ cup sugar
1 egg
⅛ teaspoon salt

Prepare brownie mix according to package directions. Spread in 9 x 13-inch baking pan and set aside. Combine cream cheese, sugar, egg, and salt for filling. Space large spoonfuls of filling on top of brownie batter. Use butter knife to form swirl designs.
Bake at 350° for 30 to 35 minutes. Cool and cut.

Frosted Banana Bars

½ cup butter or margarine, softened
1½ cups sugar
2 eggs
1 cup (8 ounces) sour cream
1 teaspoon vanilla

2 cups flour
1 teaspoon baking soda
¼ teaspoon salt
2 medium ripe bananas, mashed (about 1 cup)

In mixing bowl, cream butter and sugar. Add eggs, sour cream, and vanilla. Combine flour, baking soda, and salt; gradually add to creamed mixture. Stir in bananas. Spread into greased 15 x 10 x 1-inch baking pan. Bake at 350° for 20 to 25 minutes or until toothpick inserted near center comes out clean. Cool, then frost and cut. Store in refrigerator.

FROSTING:

1 (8 ounce) package cream cheese, softened
½ cup butter or margarine, softened

2 teaspoons vanilla
3¾ to 4 cups powdered sugar

In mixing bowl, beat cream cheese, butter, and vanilla.
Gradually beat in enough powdered sugar to achieve desired consistency.

Gumdrop Cookies

4 eggs, separated
2 cups brown sugar
1 teaspoon vanilla
½ cup nuts, chopped
1 cup orange gumdrops, finely cut
  (Assorted flavors are okay, but
  be sure to remove licorice ones.)

1 tablespoon water
2 cups flour
½ teaspoon salt
1 teaspoon baking powder

Spray 9 x 13-inch baking pan with nonstick spray, line with waxed paper, and spray waxed paper. Beat egg yolks until light and lemon colored. Add sugar and beat well. Add vanilla. Add nuts, gumdrops, and water. Sift flour, salt, and baking powder twice. Gradually add dry ingredients to gumdrop mixture. Beat egg whites until stiff. Gently fold into batter. Pour into pan. Bake at 350° for 25 minutes. While still warm, drizzle with icing. Cool and cut.

ICING:

1½ cups powdered sugar
3 tablespoons butter, softened

2 tablespoons orange juice

Mix all icing ingredients.

Honey Bars

1 egg
¾ cup vegetable oil
¼ cup honey
1 cup sugar

½ teaspoon salt
1 teaspoon cinnamon
2 cups flour
1 cup nuts, chopped

Beat egg, oil, honey, and sugar. Add salt, cinnamon, and flour. Mix well. Fold in nuts. Pat dough out on cookie sheet. Bake at 300° for 20 minutes. While hot, top with icing.

ICING:

1 cup powdered sugar
2 tablespoons milk
1 tablespoon water
2 teaspoons vanilla

Combine all icing ingredients.

Lemon Bars

CRUST:
½ cup butter, softened
¼ cup powdered sugar
1 cup flour

Cream butter and powdered sugar until fluffy. Add flour and mix well.
Spread in greased 8 x 8-inch baking pan. Bake at 350° for 12 minutes.

TOPPING:

1 cup sugar	2 tablespoons flour
2 eggs, beaten	½ teaspoon baking powder
4 tablespoons lemon juice	Powdered sugar
¼ teaspoon salt	

Beat sugar and eggs, adding in lemon juice. Add remaining ingredients and mix well.
Spread over baked crust, covering all edges. Bake at 350° for 30 minutes.
Cool and dust with powdered sugar. Cut into 1 x 2-inch rectangles.

Lemon Coconut Squares

CRUST:

1½ cups sifted flour   ½ cup butter, softened
½ cup brown sugar

Mix all crust ingredients and pat into bottom of buttered 9 x 13-inch baking pan.
Bake at 300° for 15 minutes.

FILLING:

2 eggs, beaten   2 tablespoons flour
1 cup brown sugar   ½ teaspoon baking powder
1½ cups flaked coconut   ¼ teaspoon salt
1 cup nuts, chopped   ½ teaspoon vanilla

Combine all filling ingredients and pour into baked crust. Bake at 350° for 15 minutes.

FROSTING:

1 cup powdered sugar   Juice of 1 lemon
1 tablespoon melted butter

Mix all frosting ingredients and spread over filling while still warm.

128

Magic Cookie Bars

½ cup margarine or butter
1½ cups graham cracker crumbs
1 (14 ounce) can sweetened condensed milk
1 cup semisweet chocolate chips
1⅓ cups flaked coconut
1 cup nuts, chopped

Preheat oven to 350° or 325° for glass dish. In 9 x 13-inch baking pan, melt margarine in oven. Sprinkle crumbs over margarine; mix together and press into pan. Pour condensed milk evenly over crumbs. Top evenly with remaining ingredients. Press down firmly. Bake 25 to 30 minutes or until lightly browned. Cool thoroughly before cutting.

Show Christ's love to others by giving much-needed Christmas gifts—with no name attached. Let God receive all the praise.

Dear friends, let us love one another, for love comes from God.
1 JOHN 4:7

Maple Pecan Squares

CRUST:

1 cup flour   ½ cup butter, softened
¼ cup brown sugar

Preheat oven to 350°. Mix flour, brown sugar, and butter. Press mixture firmly into 7 x 11-inch baking pan. Bake for 5 minutes. Note: Crust should not be completely cooked.

TOPPING:

⅔ cup brown sugar   ¼ teaspoon salt
1 cup maple syrup   ⅔ cup pecans, halved
2 eggs, beaten   ½ teaspoon vanilla
½ cup butter, softened   2 tablespoons flour

Combine brown sugar and syrup in saucepan. Simmer for 5 minutes. Cool slightly. Pour over beaten eggs. Stir in remaining ingredients. Spread over partially baked crust. Bake at 450° for 10 minutes, then reduce heat to 350° and bake for 20 minutes. Cool and cut into squares.

Milk Chocolate Chip and Peanut Butter Bars

½ cup butter or margarine,
 softened
½ cup creamy peanut butter
¾ cup sugar
¾ cup light brown sugar,
 packed

1 teaspoon vanilla
3 eggs
1¾ cups flour
1½ teaspoons baking powder
½ teaspoon salt
2 cups milk chocolate chips

Grease 9 x 13-inch baking pan. In large bowl, beat butter and peanut butter. Add sugars and vanilla; beat until well blended. Add eggs; beat well. Stir together flour, baking powder, and salt; add to butter mixture, beating until blended. Stir in milk chocolate chips. Spread batter in prepared pan. Bake at 350° for 40 minutes or until browned. Cool and cut into bars.

Mocha Brownies

1¼ cups semisweet chocolate chips	2 eggs
½ cup butter	¾ cup brown sugar, packed
1 teaspoon instant coffee granules	¾ cup flour
2 tablespoons hot water	½ teaspoon baking powder

In saucepan or microwave, melt chocolate chips and butter, stirring until smooth. Cool for 5 minutes. Dissolve coffee granules in hot water; set aside. In mixing bowl, beat eggs and brown sugar on medium speed for 1 minute. Stir in chocolate mixture and coffee. Combine flour and baking powder; gradually add to chocolate mixture. Pour in 9 x 13-inch baking pan. Bake at 350° for 30 to 35 minutes. Cool completely on wire rack.

FILLING:

1 tablespoon instant coffee granules	⅓ cup powdered sugar
1 tablespoon hot water	1 cup semisweet chocolate chips, melted
1 (8 ounce) package cream cheese, softened	

(cont.)

Dissolve coffee granules in water; set aside. In mixing bowl, beat cream cheese until smooth. Beat in powdered sugar, melted chocolate, and coffee. Spread over brownies.

GLAZE:
¼ cup semisweet chocolate chips
1 teaspoon shortening

Melt chocolate chips and shortening, stirring until smooth. Drizzle over filling. Refrigerate for at least 2 hours before cutting.

Peanut Butter and Jelly Bars

1 white cake mix
½ cup margarine or butter, softened
2 eggs
1 (12 ounce) jar strawberry jelly
1⅔ cups peanut butter chips

Grease 9 x 13-inch baking pan. Mix cake mix, margarine, and eggs in large bowl using spoon (mixture will be stiff). Spread evenly in pan. Spread jelly evenly on top of batter to within ½ inch of edges. Sprinkle with peanut butter chips. Bake at 375° for about 25 minutes or until golden brown around edges. Cool completely. Cut into 2½-inch bars. For ease in cutting, use sharp or wet knife.

Most brownies and baked cookies can be frozen for two to three months if sealed in airtight containers. Decorated cookies, or those low in fat, do not freeze well.

Pecan Pie Bars

CRUST:
1 yellow cake mix, divided
½ cup margarine or butter, softened
1 egg

Generously grease bottom and sides of 9 x 13-inch baking pan. Reserve ⅔ cup cake mix for filling. In large mixing bowl, combine remaining cake mix, margarine, and egg. Mix until crumbly. Press into pan. Bake at 350° for 15 to 20 minutes or until golden.

FILLING:
⅔ cup reserved cake mix
½ cup brown sugar
1½ cups dark corn syrup

1 teaspoon vanilla
3 eggs
1 cup pecans, chopped

Mix all filling ingredients except pecans and pour over partially baked crust. Sprinkle with pecans. Return to oven and bake for 30 to 35 minutes or until filling is set. Cool and cut into bars.

Peppermint Stick Bars

3 cups sugar
1 cup shortening
2 cups milk
3 cups flour

3 teaspoons baking soda
¾ cup cocoa
4 medium eggs

Cream sugar and shortening, then add milk, alternating with combined sifted flour, baking soda, and cocoa. Add eggs. Put in greased 9 x 13-inch baking pan. Bake at 300° for 30 minutes or until done.

TOPPING:

1⅔ cups white chocolate chips
4 to 6 peppermint sticks, crushed

In last 2 minutes of baking time, sprinkle white chocolate chips on top of brownies. Spread chocolate and immediately sprinkle crushed peppermint sticks on top. (If desired, substitute semisweet chocolate chips for the white.)

Spicy Pumpkin Bars

4 large eggs, beaten until frothy
1¾ cups sugar
1 cup corn oil
2 cups (16 ounces) solid-pack pumpkin
2 cups flour
2 teaspoons baking powder
1 teaspoon salt
2 teaspoons pumpkin pie spice
1 cup golden raisins

Add sugar to eggs and beat for 2 minutes. Beat in oil and pumpkin. In separate bowl,
sift dry ingredients over raisins; fold dry mixture into egg mixture.
Do not overmix. Pour into greased and floured 9 x 13-inch baking pan.
Bake at 350° for 35 to 40 minutes or until done. Cool on wire rack and cut into 24 bars.

Strawberry Linzer Bars

1¾ cups flour
½ cup sugar
1 (2 ounce) package hazelnuts or
  blanched almonds, ground (½ cup)
1 teaspoon lemon zest
½ teaspoon cinnamon
½ teaspoon baking powder
¼ teaspoon salt

½ cup butter or margarine,
  cut into pieces
1 egg, beaten
1 teaspoon vanilla
½ cup seedless strawberry or
  raspberry jam
Powdered sugar
Cinnamon

Mix flour, sugar, hazelnuts, lemon zest, cinnamon, baking powder, and salt. Add butter and beat at low speed until crumbly. Beat in egg and vanilla. Divide dough in half. Press half of dough into ungreased 9 x 9-inch baking pan. Spread jam on dough to within ½ inch of edges. Roll out other half of dough between two sheets of floured waxed paper, forming 10 x 11-inch rectangle. Remove waxed paper and cut dough into twenty ½-inch strips. Place strips over jam diagonally, forming lattice crust. Bake at 350° for 23 to 28 minutes. When cool, sprinkle with powdered sugar and cinnamon. Store in refrigerator.
Makes about 36 bars.

Jolly Jar Mix Cookies & Bars

Best of all, Christmas means a spirit of love, a time when the love of God and the love of our fellow men should prevail over all hatred and bitterness, a time when our thoughts and deeds and the spirit of our lives manifest the presence of God.
GEORGE F. McDOUGAL

Blueberry Hazelnut Dreams Mix

½ cup plus 2 tablespoons flour
½ cup rolled oats
½ cup flour
½ teaspoon baking soda
½ teaspoon salt

⅓ cup plus 1 tablespoon
brown sugar, packed
⅓ cup sugar
½ cup hazelnut pieces
½ cup dried blueberries

Layer all ingredients in 1-quart jar in order given. Attach the following recipe to jar:

BLUEBERRY HAZELNUT DREAMS
½ cup butter, softened
1 teaspoon vanilla
1 egg
Blueberry Hazelnut Dreams Mix

In medium bowl, cream together butter, vanilla, and egg. Add Blueberry Hazelnut Dreams Mix. Mix together by hand until well blended. Drop by heaping spoonfuls onto greased baking sheet. Bake at 350° for 8 to 10 minutes.

Brownie Mix

1¼ cups flour
1 teaspoon baking powder
1 teaspoon salt

⅔ cup cocoa
2¼ cups sugar
½ cup pecans, chopped

Mix together flour, baking powder, and salt in 1-quart jar. Layer remaining ingredients in order given. Press each layer firmly in place before adding next layer. Wipe out inside of jar with dry paper towel after adding cocoa so that other layers will show through the glass. Attach a tag with the following instructions:

BROWNIES
Brownie Mix
¾ cup butter, melted
4 eggs

Preheat oven to 350°. Grease and flour 9 x 13-inch baking pan. Empty Brownie Mix into large mixing bowl and stir to blend. Stir in butter and eggs. Mix thoroughly. Spread batter evenly into prepared baking pan. Bake for 25 to 30 minutes in preheated oven. Cool completely in pan before cutting into 2-inch squares.

Butter Mint Sugar Cookie Mix

1 cup sugar
1 cup soft butter mint candies,
    crushed

2½ cups flour
2 teaspoons baking powder
½ teaspoon salt

In 1-quart jar, lightly layer sugar and then candies. Combine flour, baking powder, and salt. Add flour mixture to jar. Attach a recipe card with the following instructions:

BUTTER MINT SUGAR COOKIES

1 cup butter, softened
2 large eggs
1 teaspoon vanilla
½ teaspoon butter flavoring

1 tablespoon milk
Butter Mint Sugar Cookie Mix
¼ cup sugar

Preheat oven to 350°. In large mixing bowl, beat butter until fluffy. Add eggs, vanilla, and butter flavoring, beating until blended. Stir in milk. Add Butter Mint Sugar Cookie Mix, beating well. Cover and chill dough for 1 hour. Shape dough into 1-inch balls. Roll balls in sugar. Place balls 2 inches apart on ungreased cookie sheet. Bake for 8 to 10 minutes or until barely golden. Cool for 2 minutes on cookie sheet before removing to wire rack.

Jar mixes are pretty because of their layers, but you can further dress up your canning jar gifts by cutting a piece of calico fabric with pinking shears to fit under the lid ring. You can also add multiple ribbons to the lid to hold the recipes. If you feel you need further embellishments, you can paint the outside of the jar with craft paint or the inside of the jar with melted chocolate.

Butterscotch Brownie Mix

2 cups flour
1½ tablespoons baking powder
¼ teaspoon salt

½ cup flaked coconut
¾ cup pecans, chopped
2 cups brown sugar, packed

To 1-liter glass jar, add flour, baking powder, and salt; stir together and pack down.
Then add and pack down remaining ingredients in order given.
Attach a label with the following instructions:

BUTTERSCOTCH BROWNIES
Butterscotch Brownie Mix
¾ cup butter, softened
2 eggs, beaten
2 teaspoons vanilla

Preheat oven to 375°. Grease 9 x 13-inch baking pan. Empty Butterscotch Brownie Mix
into large mixing bowl; stir to break up lumps. Add butter, eggs, and vanilla; mix until
well blended. Spread batter evenly in prepared pan. Bake for 25 minutes.
Allow to cool in pan before cutting into squares.

Chocolate Chip Cookie Mix

¾ cup sugar
½ cup brown sugar, packed
1¾ cups flour

¾ teaspoon baking soda
½ teaspoon salt
1½ cups semisweet chocolate chips

In 1-quart glass jar, layer ingredients in order given, combining flour, baking soda, and salt before adding to jar. Attach a recipe card with the following instructions:

CHOCOLATE CHIP COOKIES

Chocolate Chip Cookie Mix
¾ cup shortening
2 tablespoons milk

½ tablespoon vanilla
½ teaspoon butter flavoring
1 egg

Preheat oven to 350°. In large mixing bowl, empty Chocolate Chip Cookie Mix, stirring to combine. Add shortening, milk, vanilla, butter flavoring, and egg. Beat with spoon or electric mixer until well blended. Drop by rounded tablespoonfuls 2 inches apart onto ungreased cookie sheet. Bake for 11 to 13 minutes or until light brown.
Cool for 1 minute on cookie sheet before removing to wire rack.

Cookie swap with other bakers in your family. Have each participant bake his or her favorite Christmas cookie recipe, baking enough to give a dozen away to others. You'll all end up with a tasty variety of holiday treats—without going to the trouble of purchasing ingredients for different recipes.

Cookie Jar Sugar Cookie Mix

4 cups flour
1 teaspoon baking powder
½ teaspoon baking soda

½ teaspoon salt
¾ tablespoon nutmeg
1½ cups sugar

Combine flour with baking powder, baking soda, salt, and nutmeg. In clean 1-liter glass jar with wide mouth, layer sugar and then flour mixture. Press firmly in place and seal. Attach a recipe card with the following instructions:

COOKIE JAR SUGAR COOKIES

1 egg
1 cup butter or margarine,
   softened

½ cup sour cream
1 teaspoon vanilla
Sugar Cookie Mix

In large bowl, beat egg with butter until light and fluffy. At low speed of electric mixer, add sour cream, vanilla, and Sugar Cookie Mix. Mix until combined, using hands if necessary. Cover dough and refrigerate for several hours or overnight. Remove dough from refrigerator. Preheat oven to 375°. Roll out chilled dough on lightly floured surface to ⅛-inch thickness. Cut into desired shapes. Place on ungreased cookie sheet and bake for 10 to 12 minutes.

Loaded Oatmeal Raisin Cookie Mix

1 cup flour
1 teaspoon baking soda
1 teaspoon cinnamon
½ teaspoon nutmeg
½ teaspoon ground cloves
½ teaspoon salt

¾ cup brown sugar, packed
½ cup sugar
½ cup raisins
1 cup quick-cooking oats
½ cup almonds, sliced
½ cup butterscotch chips

In bowl, combine first six ingredients. Pour flour mixture into 1-quart glass jar and continue layering in order given. Attach a recipe card with the following instructions:

LOADED OATMEAL RAISIN COOKIES

¾ cup butter, softened
1 egg

1 teaspoon vanilla
Loaded Oatmeal Raisin Cookie Mix

Preheat oven to 350°. In mixing bowl, cream butter. Beat in egg and vanilla. Add Loaded Oatmeal Raisin Cookie Mix and mix well. Drop by rounded teaspoonfuls 2 inches apart onto greased cookie sheet. Bake for 9 to 11 minutes or until golden brown. Cool for 2 minutes on cookie sheet before removing to wire rack.

Molasses Cookie Mix

2 cups flour
1 teaspoon baking soda
1 teaspoon cinnamon
¼ teaspoon ground cloves
1 teaspoon ginger

1 cup sugar
1 teaspoon baking powder
½ teaspoon nutmeg
⅛ teaspoon allspice

In 1-quart glass jar, layer ingredients in order given. Attach the following recipe to jar:

MOLASSES COOKIES

¾ cup butter or margarine,
softened
¼ cup sulfured molasses

1 egg
Molasses Cookie Mix
Sugar

Preheat oven to 375°. In large bowl, mix butter, molasses, and egg. Add Molasses Cookie Mix; beat until smooth. Shape dough into 1-inch balls. Roll in sugar. Place 2 inches apart on ungreased cookie sheets. Bake for 9 to 11 minutes. Cool on wire racks.

Peanut Butter and Chocolate Cookie Mix

¾ cup sugar
1¾ cups flour
½ teaspoon baking soda
½ cup brown sugar

1 teaspoon baking powder
8 peanut butter cups, chopped
    into chunks

In 1-quart glass jar, layer ingredients in order given. Attach the following recipe to jar:

PEANUT BUTTER AND CHOCOLATE COOKIES

Peanut Butter and Chocolate
    Cookie Mix
½ cup butter, softened

1 teaspoon vanilla
1 egg, slightly beaten

Sift out peanut butter cup chunks and set aside. Empty remaining cookie mix into large mixing bowl and stir with fork. Add butter, vanilla, and egg. Mix until completely blended. Mix in peanut butter cup chunks. Shape into 1½-inch balls. Place 2 inches apart on greased cookie sheets. Bake at 375° for 12 to 14 minutes. Cool for 5 minutes on baking sheet. Remove cookies to racks to finish cooling.

Triple Chocolate Chunk Cookie Mix

½ cup sugar
¾ cup brown sugar, packed
1¾ cups flour
1 teaspoon baking soda
½ teaspoon salt

⅓ cup cocoa
4 ounces white chocolate chunks
½ cup milk chocolate chips
⅓ cup semisweet chocolate chips

In a 1-quart glass jar, layer ingredients in order given, combining flour, baking soda, and salt. Attach a recipe card with the following instructions:

TRIPLE CHOCOLATE CHUNK COOKIES

Triple Chocolate Chunk
Cookie Mix
1 cup butter, softened

1 teaspoon vanilla
2 eggs

Preheat oven to 325°. Carefully remove semisweet chocolate chips, milk chocolate chips, and white chocolate chunks from Triple Chocolate Chunk Cookie Mix; set aside. In mixing bowl, beat butter, vanilla, and eggs until creamy. In large bowl, empty remaining contents of cookie mix, stirring to combine; add to creamed mixture until well blended. Stir in chocolate chips and white chocolate chunks. Drop by rounded tablespoonfuls onto ungreased cookie sheet. Bake for 11 to 13 minutes or until cookies are set and appear dry. Cool for 1 minute on cookie sheet before removing to wire rack.

Tropical Jewel Cookie Mix

1¾ cups flour
1 teaspoon baking powder
½ teaspoon baking soda
½ teaspoon salt
½ teaspoon allspice
¾ cup brown sugar, packed

⅓ cup sugar
½ cup semisweet chocolate chips
½ cup white baking chips
½ cup flaked coconut
⅓ cup dried pineapple, chopped
⅓ cup macadamia nuts, chopped

Combine flour, baking powder, baking soda, salt, and allspice. Place in bottom of 1-quart glass jar. Layer remaining ingredients in order given. Attach a recipe card with the following instructions:

TROPICAL JEWEL COOKIES

Tropical Jewel Cookie Mix
½ cup ripe banana, mashed
1 egg

½ cup butter, softened
1 teaspoon vanilla

Preheat oven to 375°. In large bowl, empty Tropical Jewel Cookie Mix, stirring to combine. Add banana, egg, butter, and vanilla. Beat with spoon until well blended. Drop by rounded tablespoonfuls 2 inches apart onto ungreased cookie sheet. Bake for 10 to 12 minutes or until lightly browned. Cool for 2 minutes on cookie sheet before removing to wire rack.

White Chocolate Cranberry Cookie Mix

½ cup brown sugar, packed
½ cup sugar
1 cup flour
1 teaspoon baking powder
¼ teaspoon baking soda

¼ teaspoon salt
1 cup old-fashioned oats
4 ounces white chocolate
  baking bar, chopped
½ cup dried cranberries

In 1-quart widemouthed glass jar, layer ingredients in order given, combining flour, baking powder, baking soda, and salt. Attach a recipe card with the following instructions:

WHITE CHOCOLATE CRANBERRY COOKIES

White Chocolate Cranberry
  Cookie Mix
⅔ cup butter, softened

1 large egg
½ tablespoon vanilla

Preheat oven to 375°. Carefully remove cranberries and white chocolate from White Chocolate Cranberry Cookie Mix; set aside. In large mixing bowl, empty remaining contents of cookie mix. Add butter, egg, and vanilla. Beat with electric mixer until well blended. Stir in white chocolate and cranberries. Drop by rounded tablespoonfuls 2 inches apart onto ungreased cookie sheet. Bake for 10 minutes or until lightly browned. Cool for 2 minutes on cookie sheet before removing to wire rack.

Cookie Baking Reference

Drop style at 350° to 400° for 8 to 15 minutes
Rolled and cut at 350° to 375° for 5 to 12 minutes
Refrigerated at 350° to 400° for 8 to 15 minutes
Filled at 350° to 375° for 8 to 12 minutes
Bars at 325° to 375° for 10 to 35 minutes

Index

Also Available from Mary & Martha. . .

In the Kitchen with Mary & Martha
ISBN 1-59310-878-8

One-Dish Wonders
ISBN 1-59789-011-1

Cookin' Up Christmas
ISBN 1-59789-239-4

224 pages • hardback with printed comb binding
Available Wherever Books Are Sold